# NATIVE AMERICAN RIGHTS THE DECADES OLD FIGHT

## CIVIL RIGHTS BOOKS FOR CHILDREN CHILDREN'S HISTORY BOOKS

Speedy Publishing LLC

40 E. Main St. #1156

Newark, DE 19711

www.speedypublishing.com

Copyright 2017

In this book, you will learn about Native American Indians, who they are, where they lived, how they lived, and how they have struggled for their civil rights since the arrival of the Europeans.

# WHO WERE THE NATIVE AMERICAN INDIANS?

Native American Indians are grouped into tribes or nations by using specific classifications.

Tribes shared similar religious beliefs, culture, social structure and other unique characteristics that made them different from other early civilizations. There are more than one thousand (1,000) tribes in the United States. These tribes differ because of some social behaviors and more importantly Language, such as the Apache Indians and tribes from the Great Plains.

# NATIVE INDIAN COMMUNITY

# CLASSIFICATION INTO REGIONS

Surviving the most treacherous winters in the USA, they have been classified based on regions they have lived in over time.

The Mohave, Miwok and Intuit tribes of Alaska are just some of the tribes that we have included in this classification. The Great Basin, consisting of the Washo, Ute and Shoshone tribes, was considered a parched area and one of the last tribes to interact with the Europeans.

UTE'S CHIEF AND FAMILY

One of the biggest areas and most famous tribes known for hunting bison. The Great Plains, were wandering people, lived in teepees and followed herds of bison. Great Plains tribes consisted of Blackfoot, Arapahoe, Cheyenne, Comanche and Crow.

THE VILLAGE OF CHEYENNE

The Iroquois Indians of New York, the Shawnee, and the Wappani made up the Northeast WoodLands. The Northwest Coast/PLateau houses and totem poLes were made of cedar.

The Tlingit, Salish, and Nez Perce tribes called this area home. The Cherokee, the biggest Native American tribe, lived in the Southeast region.

The Florida Seminole and the Chickasaw were considered a part of the Cherokee tribe. They were accomplished farmers and inclined not to roam. Consisting of The Navajo Nation, Apache, and Pueblo Indians, the Southwest region was an arid land and the tribes that lived here lived in homes built with adobe bricks. They were the famed tribes living in this area.

**NAVAJO MEN**

# OTHER GROUPS

The Algonquian was a significant group of more than 100 tribes speaking Algonquian.

## THE ALGONQUIANS

They encompassed the country and included the Blackfeet, Cheyenne, Mohicans, and Ottawa tribe. The Apaches spoke Apache and were a band of six tribes.

Five Native American tribes, the Cayuga, Oneida, Mohawk, Onondaga, and the Seneca made up the Iroquois League, and later joined with the Tuscarora nation.

The northeastern area of the United States consisted of these nations. The Great Sioux Nation consisted of peoples generally called Sioux. They separated into three groups: Lakota, Western Dakota, and Eastern Dakota. Great Plains Indians were made up of the Sioux.

THE GREAT SIOUX NATION

# BASIC LIFE OF THE NATIVE AMERICAN INDIAN

A Lot of their clothing was made using Buckskin, a smooth Leather usually created from skin of a deer, elk, or moose.

They wore **Moccasins** which were shoes created from supple leather worn by several Native American men.

A porcupine roach, is a headdress made from animal hair that would stick straight up above the head.

They would occasionally use Wampum, beads consisting of shells, for money. To get around, they used Canoes, a thin boat with pointy ends and paddles, to move through waters.

WAMPUM BEADS

They also used a Travois, made from long poles and pulled by horses or dogs, to carry items when relocating.

They would create Totem poles, a tall post made of wood and engraved with symbols, representing various meanings, stories, or important events.

# LIVING CONDITIONS

They lived on land called a reservation which was land put aside by the United States to be managed by Native American tribes.

A COMMON SHELTER USED BY INDIGENOUS PEOPLE IN CANADA.

Their homes consisted of Chickees, Igloos, Teepees, and Wigwams. Built by the Seminole Indians of Florida, a Chickee is a dwelling with a floor that is raised, covered by a thatch roof, with open sides.

The Intuit tribe of the Artic Lived in IgLoos formed with snow and ice. Made from poLLs covered by buffaLo hide, Teepees would Look Like a cone that was upside down.

**Teepees** were used by plains Indians since they were easily moved. Covered by tree bark and made with wooden poles, a Wigwam was a dome shaped home.

# TEEPEES

# SPIRITUALITY

The **Medicine Man** was known as the spiritual or religious spearhead. If a person wanted to look for their life purpose and spiritual direction they would hold a ceremony called a **Vision Quest**.

# MEDICINE MAN

A spiritual movement predicting an end to the development of the white peoples was known as the Ghost Dance.

A Powwow was a simple ritual or assembly held between Native American Indians.

# ARRIVAL OF THE EUROPEANS

When the Europeans arrived to America, they brought disease which killed most of the natives and their lives were forever changed.

NATIVE AMERICANS AND EUROPEANS FIRST CONTACT.

They decided they wanted to launch their private government and conquer their land and the tribes were forced west. The Native Americans were unable to fight back against the dangerous weapons and numbers of these newcomers.

Once the Indian Removal Act was signed by President Jackson in 1830, the Indians are forced out. Five Tribes, consisting of the Choctaw, Seminole, Creek, Chickasaw, and Cherokee tribes, were forced to relocate from Southeastern United States to Oklahoma Indian Territory.

In 1838, some tribes Located in southeast U.S. were forced to reLocate to OkLahoma. This came to be known as the Trail of Tears because thousands of Cherokee peoples Lost their Lives. The United States established treaties with various Native American tribes until 1871.

TRAIL OF TEARS
Bell Removal Route

On October 11, 1838, the last group of 650-700 treaty party Cherokees (so-called), led by conductor John A. Bell, also Cherokee, left Ft. Cass in Charleston, TN, headed for their new homes in the West. With them was U.S. Army LT. Edward Deas, military escort and disbursement officer. They were given rations in 5-day increments. From October 23-26, they were camped at "The Head of Battle Creek" (Martin Springs) and on the Cumberland Mountain in the Trussell Point Area. On the 26th, they were issued rations, and purchased corn and fodder from Benjamin Trussell for their 318 horses. They continued through present-day Monteagle, Sewanee, St. Mary's, and Cowan to Winchester, then followed the route of present-day Hwy. 64 to Memphis and then on to Arkansas. The group suffered 23 deaths, including 2 infants, on the 89-day, 707 mile Journey. On Jan. 7, 1839, they arrived at Vineyard, AR, where they disbanded near the post office just West of present-day Evansville. In spite of removal, many Cherokee remain in Tennessee.

THIS MARKER MADE POSSIBLE BY THE TRAIL OF TEARS REMEMBRANCE MOTORCYCLE RIDE.

TO
INTERSTATE
24

NORTH
41

SCHOOL
SPEED
LIMIT
15

# THE STRUGGLE FOR THEIR CIVIL RIGHTS

◇◇◇◇◇◇◇◇◇◇◇◇

The tribes then became accepted as independent populations once the Indian Appropriations Act of 1871 was signed, holding that these tribes no longer were believed to be nations and the prior treaties were not considered valid.

A NATIVE AMERICAN CHIEF

As time went on, their life didn't improve. They were required to reside on reservations, and still lost land through policies created by the United States, including the new act titled General Allotment Act of 1887.

They continued to experience a life of poverty, employment was low and education was poor. Even though the fourteenth amendment of the Constitution considers all people born of the U.S. as citizens, they were still not considered as citizens, and still not permitted to vote.

The Indian Citizen Act was enacted in 1924, thus providing them citizenship in the United States, as well as voting rights, although some states continued the practice of not allowing Indians to vote until 1948.

# THE INDIAN CITIZEN ACT 1924

Sometime in the 1900s, Life improved for the Native Americans. The Indian Reorganization Act became effective in 1934. This Act reversed some issues with previous Laws and renewed the rights of the Indians to establish their own governments.

Life as they knew it began improving and in 1968, the Indian Civil Rights Act was signed into Law. Followed the next year when, in 1969, the National Indian Education Association was formed to enrich the education of Native Americans.

This was also known as the Indian Bill of Rights and this law ensured their civil rights. This law ensures many of the same rights that are contained in the Bill of Rights. These rights include the freedom of speech, the right to a fair and speedy trial, due process and jury trial, the right to have an attorney, freedom with the press and more. The Indian Bill of Rights was a vital law and a major advancement for Native American civil rights.

SITTING BULL AND BUFFALO BILL 1885

Since people reside on reservations are considered as dual citizens, there are many intricate issues surrounding their civil rights. As well as being citizens of the United States, they are also considered a tribal nation. Current issues include but are not limited to, their right to vote and sports teams using Native American likenesses as mascots.

This is a brief introduction into the history of the Native American Indians and their struggle for their civil rights. We know that you will have fun researching this topic on the internet, at the library, and by asking your parents and teachers.

Visit
BABY PROFESSOR
EDUCATION KIDS
www.BabyProfessorBooks.com
to download Free Baby Professor eBooks
and view our catalog of new and exciting
Children's Books